LIFE STORY

SNAKE

MICHAEL CHINERY

Photography by
Barrie Watts

Illustrated by
Denys Ovenden

Troll Associates

Library of Congress Cataloging-in-Publication Data

Chinery, Michael.
    Snake / by Michael Chinery; photography by Barrie Watts;
illustrated by Denys Ovenden.
       p.   cm.—(Life story)
    Summary: An introduction to the physical characteristics, habits,
and natural environment of snakes.
    ISBN 0-8167-2106-8 (lib. bdg.)   ISBN 0-8167-2107-6 (pbk.)
    1. Snakes—Juvenile literature. [1. Snakes.] I. Watts, Barrie,
ill. II. Ovenden, Denys, ill. III. Title. IV. Series: Chinery,
Michael. Life story.
QL666.O6C53 1991
597.96—dc20   90-10951

Published by Troll Associates, Mahwah, New Jersey 07430

Designed by James Marks

Printed in the U.S.A.

10 9 8 7 6 5 4 3 2 1

INTRODUCTION

Snakes have no legs, but they manage
very well without them. This book tells
you about the North American corn
snake that some people keep as a pet.
You can find out how the snake uses
its scales for moving and how it smells
with its tongue. You can also discover
how a snake opens its mouth wide
enough to swallow animals bigger
than itself. Learn how the baby snakes
slice open their tough eggshells so that
they can get out, and see how they
change their skins every now and then
as they grow up.

This colorful snake is a North American corn snake. When you see it coiled up like this, it is hard to imagine that it has a sturdy backbone inside it.

The backbone is actually made up of more than 200 small bones called vertebrae, joined together like a string of beads. There are flexible joints between them, so the backbone can be bent and coiled just like that string of beads.

4

Snakes don't have any eyelids. The
animals do a lot of burrowing, or
digging in the earth, and if they had
eyelids they would have to keep their
eyes closed to keep dirt out. Instead of
eyelids, a snake has a tough, clear scale
over each eye, called a spectacle. The
spectacle gets scratched, but the snake
gets a new one from time to time. A
snake's eyesight is not really very good.
Like most snakes, the corn snake
depends more on smell than on sight.

6

This corn snake is exploring with its forked tongue. As it moves forward, the snake flicks its tongue out every few seconds and taps it on the ground to pick up scents or smells. The tongue carries these back to a special area in the roof of the mouth, which sorts out the different smells and tells the snake what is going on around it.

If the snake picks up the scent of a mouse or rat, it will follow the trail until it finds the animal. Then it will have a tasty meal.

The snake's body is covered with tough scales. The scales on the belly are as wide as the body. They help the snake to move. The snake uses its muscles to move these scales forward in groups. Then it digs the edges of its scales lightly into the ground.

Muscles fixed to the scales then pull the snake's body forward smoothly in a straight line. But this is only one way of moving. More often the snake wriggles from side to side.

10

This snake is changing its skin. This is called molting. Snakes do this up to seven times in a year, because their outer skin wears out as they slither over the ground or as they grow larger.

When it's time to molt, the snake usually finds a safe place to hide. Its colors become dull as the worn-out skin separates from the lower layers, and its eyes cloud over until it is almost blind. A new outer skin is already growing under the old one.

After a few days the old skin splits, and the snake wriggles out of it. The snake is now back to its proper color. It also has bright new spectacles over its eyes. The old skin is left behind like a ghost.

Snakes are meat-eaters. The corn snake feeds mainly on rats and mice, which it tracks down by scent. When it gets close enough to the animal it wants to eat – its prey – the snake moves forward at high speed and grabs its victim in its mouth. At the same time, the snake coils its body tightly around its victim. It does not crush the animal, but stops it from breathing.

When the victim is dead, the snake starts to swallow it. The prey is swallowed whole, for the snake's spiky teeth are made only for catching and holding things. They can't cut or chew anything.

The snake's prey looks much too big to be swallowed, but snakes have very unusual jaws. They can easily swallow animals fatter than themselves. The jawbones are only loosely joined to each other, and the skin around the snake's mouth and throat stretches easily. This lets the snake open its mouth very wide.

Using its backward-pointing teeth, it slowly drags the prey into its mouth. The prey is usually swallowed head first because it goes down more easily that way. The snake can take an hour or more to swallow a rat.

Corn snakes generally mate in the spring. The male tracks down the female by her smell. He strokes her with his chin before coiling his body around her and mating with her.

Between mating and laying the eggs, the female likes to bask in the sunshine. The warmth helps the eggs to develop inside her body.

18

In a few weeks when she is ready to lay her eggs, the female corn snake looks for a damp spot in which to burrow. She may tunnel into or under rotten wood, but she sometimes takes over the burrow of a mouse or some other small animal.

She lays up to 24 leathery eggs in the burrow. Each egg is about one inch long when it is laid. It swells as the baby snake grows inside it and it may be an inch and a half long just before it hatches. Plenty of animals like to eat snakes' eggs. The female corn snake stays close to her eggs to keep these enemies away.

The eggs are ready to hatch about 8 to 12 weeks after they were laid, although they will take a bit longer in cold weather. The baby snake starts to cut slits in the leathery eggshell. It uses a special egg tooth on its upper lip.

The tooth has razor-sharp edges, but cutting through the shell is still hard work for a little snake. The snake takes plenty of rests before finally pushing its head out. The egg tooth has no more work to do and soon falls off.

This baby corn snake in the photograph is nearly ready to leave its eggshell. It might sit looking out like this for several hours while it builds up its strength.

Its tongue is picking up scents that tell it what is happening around it. Once the baby wriggles out of its eggshell, it will have to look after itself. Its mother doesn't help it at all.

This newly hatched snake is as thick as a pencil and about 12 inches long. It is amazing to think that it just came out of an egg only an inch and a half long.

The baby will slowly turn rusty brown like its mother. If it escapes from foxes and birds of prey, it can live for about ten years and reach a length of three feet or more. The biggest corn snakes are about six feet long.

The corn snake lives mainly on the ground, but it is very good at climbing trees. It can go almost straight up a tree trunk by digging the edges of its scales into cracks in the bark. Even very young snakes know how to do this.

Corn snakes are also good swimmers, although they usually live in dry fields and bushy places. But no matter where snakes live, they are an important part of our natural world.

Fascinating facts

Anaconda

One of the world's largest snakes is the anaconda. It lives in South America and reaches lengths of more than 24 feet. It can even swallow a pig!

The world's smallest snakes are the thread snakes, which live in Africa, southern Asia, south-western North America, and tropical areas of Central and South America. They are no more than about five inches long and can squeeze through holes only an eighth of an inch wide. They feed mainly on ants.

Poisonous snakes kill their prey by injecting poison into them through special teeth called fangs.

The spitting cobra is a very poisonous snake, but it doesn't have to bite to be dangerous. It fires jets of poison which can blind other animals if it gets into their eyes. The cobra uses this habit mainly to defend itself.

The world's most poisonous land snakes are the smooth-scaled snake and the tiger snake, both of which live in Australia.

Spitting cobra

Index

anaconda 30
ants 30

baby snake 3, 20, 22, 24, 26
backbone 4
birds 26
bones 4
burrowing 6, 20

climbing 28
color 12

eggs 18, 20, 22, 24, 26
eggshell 3, 22, 24
egg tooth 22
enemies 20
eyelids 6
eyes 6, 12

fangs 31
feeding 8, 14, 16
foxes 26

hatching 22, 24, 26

jaws 16
joints 4

mating 18
molting 12
mouse 8, 14, 20
mouth 3, 8, 16
moving 10

muscles 10

pig 30
poisonous snakes 31
prey 14, 16

rat 8, 14, 16

scales 3, 6, 10, 28
sight 6
skin 12, 16
smell 3, 6, 8, 14, 18, 24
smooth-scaled snake 31
spectacle 6, 12
spitting cobra 31
swallowing 14, 16
swimming 28

teeth 14, 16, 22, 31
thread snake 30
tiger snake 31
tongue 3, 8, 24

vertebrae 4